HELEN KELLER & ANNIE SULLIVAN
WORKING MIRACLES TOGETHER

BY

Jon Zonderman

Illustrations by Jerry Harston

A BLACKBIRCH PRESS BOOK

WOODBRIDGE, CONNECTICUT

Published by Blackbirch Press, Inc.
One Bradley Road
Woodbridge , CT 06525

Printed in Hong Kong

10 9 8 7 6 5 4 3 2 1

Library of Congress Cataloging-in-Publication Data

Zonderman, Jon.
    Helen Keller and Annie Sullivan, working miracles together / by Jon Zonderman. — 1st ed.
        p.   cm. — (Partners)
    Includes bibliographical references and index.
    ISBN 1-56711-088-6   ISBN 1-56711-119-X (Pbk.)
    1. Keller, Helen, 1880–1968—Juvenile literature. 2. Blind-deaf-United States—Biography—Juvenile literature. 3. Sullivan, Annie, 1866–1936—Juvenile literature. 4. Teachers of the blind-deaf-United States—Biography—Juvenile literature. [1. Keller, Helen, 1880–1968. 2. Blind. 3. Deaf. 4. Physically handicapped. 5. Sullivan, Annie, 1866–1936. 6. Teachers. 7. Women—Biography.] I. Title. II. Series.
    HV1624.K4Z66 1994
    362.4'1'092—dc20
    [B]   94-20126
                                                                                        CIP
                                                                                         AC

○ ○ ○ ○ ○ Contents ○ ○ ○ ○ ○

When Annie Sullivan and Helen Keller first met, they battled each other all the time. Soon, however, they grew to love and respect each other.

 ○ ○ ○ ○ ○ **1** ○ ○ ○ ○ ○

Helen and Teacher

When a special teacher from Boston named
Annie Mansfield Sullivan first arrived in
Tuscumbia, Alabama, in March of 1887, she
found a 6-year-old, half-wild child was to
be her new student. Not only could the
young Helen Keller not see, hear, or speak,
but she was nearly uncontrollable.

Helen Keller was born a normal child. But
before her second birthday, she was struck with a
mysterious illness. Although her high fever went
away, it was clear to her parents that she never really
recovered.

Until Annie Sullivan arrived, Helen's parents
thought she would spend her life in their care. They

believed their only task was simply to see that their daughter was fed and that she hurt herself as little as possible.

Annie, who had severe problems with her own eyesight and had received little education until she was a teenager, believed Helen had the same ability to learn as any child. The key, she thought, would be finding a way to communicate with the little girl.

The Normal Learning Process

Boys and girls who can see and hear, learn how to communicate as a natural part of their early development. Most children begin to speak when they are between 1 and 1 1/2 years old. Even young babies hear the sounds their parents and others make. At a few months of age, they usually begin testing their voices in an effort to imitate speech.

At the same time that babies with normal sight and hearing are seeing objects, they are also hearing words. And as children begin speaking, they begin to learn the words for objects they use.

For a child who cannot see, making the first connections between words, speech, and objects in the world is more difficult. For a child who cannot hear, developing language takes even more time. Sign language or, in some cases, lip reading can help these children to communicate. Some can learn to speak by touching a person's throat to feel the vibrations and watching the shape that a person's mouth makes when a particular sound is made.

A blind-and-deaf child will have an especially difficult time learning how to communicate, since he or she cannot imitate sounds or see sign language. Teaching a child like this to communicate is an enormous and time-consuming task.

Today, most deaf-and-blind children get special education. But 100 years ago—when Helen was born—such children's families were ill-equipped to educate them. Often, these children were put in an institution for the "feeble-minded."

Annie Sullivan found a troubled and frustrated child when she arrived at the Keller home in 1887. Stubborn and used to getting her own way, Helen fought Annie at every turn. Even feeding became a battleground. Sometimes Helen did not get fed because she refused to use her fork or put

Annie Sullivan found a frustrated and severely troubled child at the Keller home in 1887.

her napkin on her lap. It hurt Helen's parents to watch this, and many times they left the dining room. In the meantime, Helen and Annie spent hours trying to get through a meal. Annie's efforts to get Helen to wash, comb her hair, or button her clothes often took an equally long time.

As much as it pained Helen's parents to watch their daughter fight, they understood that they had to let Annie try to give Helen some of the tools for living that they could not. And partly because they could not stand to watch their daughter cry—especially Mr. Keller—they let Annie and Helen move out of the main house to a small cottage on the farm.

Although Annie did not want to break her young student's spirit—a spirit that kept such a girl from becoming completely helpless—she felt that Helen could not move forward until she understood that there were rules for living, even for people who had disabilities.

After Annie had established with Helen that she was not going to tolerate what Helen's parents had, Annie began to fingerspell into Helen's palm. Fingerspelling is similar to sign language, but the symbols for each letter are made against the palm

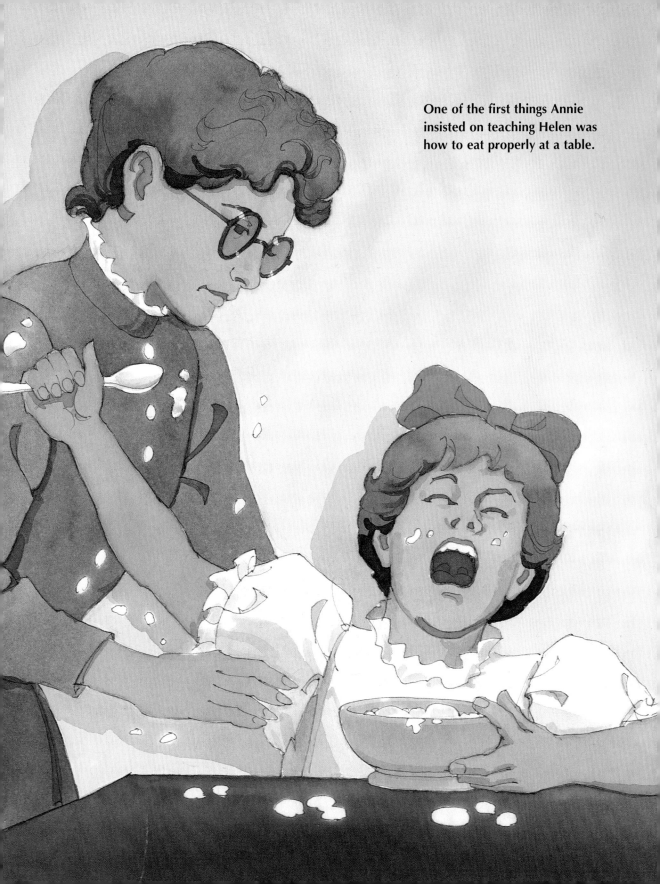

One of the first things Annie insisted on teaching Helen was how to eat properly at a table.

of the hand. This way, a blind-and-deaf individual can sense the shape of each letter instead of seeing it. Helen began to copy Annie's technique, her fingers flying in Annie's hand. But it was still a game to Helen. As Annie wrote to a friend shortly after she and Helen moved into the cottage, "she has no idea yet that everything has a name."

While Helen was years behind her age in language skills, her mind had been developing and was ready to grasp complicated concepts. So when the moment came that Helen finally realized how each object had a name, she became at once excited and incredibly curious.

That moment occurred on April 5, 1887, less than three weeks after Annie's arrival. While

Helen had a major learning breakthrough when she realized that the cool, wet liquid she felt one day at the well had a name: "w-a-t-e-r."

drawing water from the well, Annie put Helen's hand under the stream and spelled into her other palm, "w-a-t-e-r." Helen later wrote in her autobiography, "I knew that w-a-t-e-r meant the wonderful, cool something that was flowing over my hand. Everything had a name and each name gave birth to a new thought. As I returned to the house, every object seemed to quiver to life."

After learning the names of half a dozen objects, Helen pointed to Annie, and Annie spelled "t-e-a-c-h-e-r" into the little girl's hand. From then on, Helen always referred to Annie as "teacher."

For the next 50 years, Helen Keller and her "teacher" from Boston were inseparable. As they learned from each other, they grew together with both their hearts and minds. As constant partners, they formed a deep love and understanding for one another that few people have equalled since.

"Everything had a name and each name gave birth to a new thought. As I returned to the house, every object seemed to quiver to life," Helen remembered in her autobiography.

Alabama Homestead, Massachusetts Poorhouse

 Helen Adams Keller was born on June 27, 1880, the first child of Kate and Arthur Keller. Mr. Keller, known as Captain Keller because of his rank in the Confederate Army during the Civil War, was the owner, publisher, and editor of the *North Alabamian*, a weekly newspaper based in Tuscumbia, where the family lived. The Keller family was well off. Mr. Keller owned many acres of farmland in addition to the newspaper.

Helen was a normal child at birth—her parents even believed she was exceptional. But at 19 months of age, she contracted a fever. After the fever went away, the formerly quiet and happy girl began sleeping fitfully, turning away from sunlight, and crying often.

It was clear to her parents that their little girl, who was already speaking and loved to run and play, was losing her eyesight and her hearing. Doctors today believe Helen Keller's illness was scarlet fever, although her doctors in 1882 knew little about the problem.

Whatever the actual illness, it left Helen alone in a dark and silent world. Later, in her autobiography, Helen described her early self as "a phantom." At the age of 2, she had quickly stopped learning new words and then forgot how to speak at all.

Because she had lost her sight and hearing after beginning to develop language, Helen developed a kind of primitive sign language: a shake of the head meant "no;" a nod meant "yes;" a pull meant "come with me;" and a push meant "go away." She would imitate spreading butter on bread when she was hungry, and would turn an imaginary crank if she wanted her mother to make ice cream for dessert.

By age 5, Helen had a "vocabulary" of about 50 gestures, though the only sounds she made were

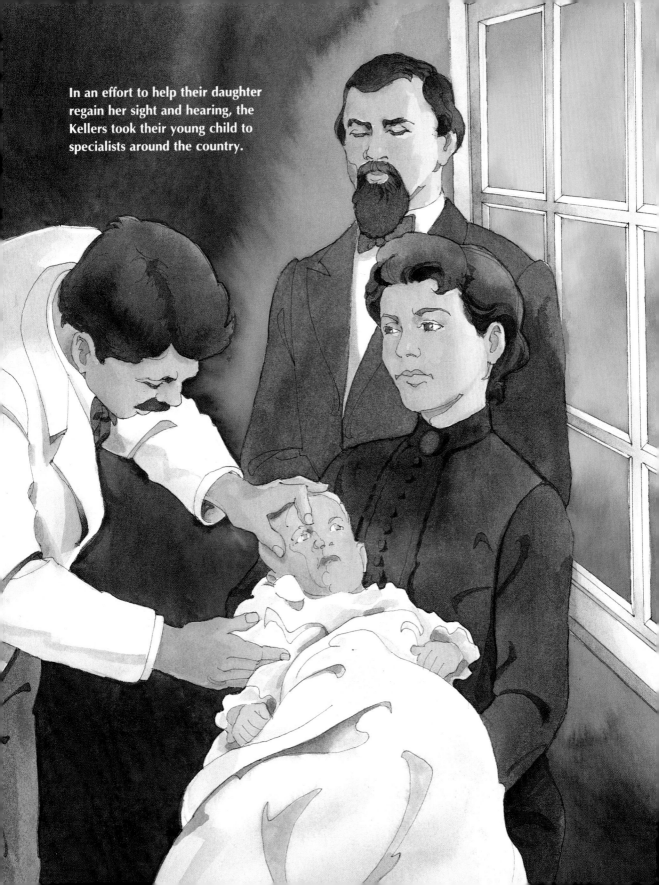

In an effort to help their daughter regain her sight and hearing, the Kellers took their young child to specialists around the country.

squeals of pleasure or cries of pain. Her difficulty communicating made her angry, and she often threw temper tantrums. It seemed that Helen was always either angry or pouting, and that she had very little patience. Most family members suggested that she be committed to the state home for the mentally ill. But Helen's parents vowed to find a way to educate their special daughter. Mrs. Keller thought she might have found the way when she read *American Notes*, by the English author Charles Dickens, in which he described his first meeting in 1842 with a deaf-and-blind woman named Laura Bridgman.

The Story of Laura

Laura had also lost her sight and hearing at a young age. For years, she had lived in a dark and silent world like Helen's. Then Laura was sent to the famous Perkins School for the Blind in Boston. There, she met Samuel Gridley Howe, a teacher and director of the Perkins School. He taught Laura how to communicate using the manual alphabet—letters traced on the palm of her hand.

While Kate Keller was thinking about the possibilities of teaching Helen with the manual alphabet, she and her husband were also taking Helen to see many specialists in the fields of eyesight and hearing. They traveled as far as Baltimore, where a doctor confirmed that Helen would be blind and deaf for life. The doctor, however, suggested to the Kellers that they go to Washington, D.C., to see the famous inventor Alexander Graham Bell.

Bell is best known as the inventor of the telephone, among many other creations. Few people know, however, that Bell's desire to invent the telephone grew out of his efforts to teach deaf children to speak.

Bell knew of Laura Bridgman, and suggested that the Kellers contact Michael Anagnos, the current Perkins School director in Massachusetts. Anagnos found young Helen's case interesting because of its similarities to that of Laura Bridgman's, who was a middle-aged woman, but still lived

The famous inventor, Alexander Graham Bell, worked with the Kellers to find help for Helen.

at the Perkins School. He soon wrote to the Kellers that he was sending a special teacher to Alabama who would work with Helen.

The young woman Anagnos chose was Annie Sullivan. Annie had studied for many years at the Perkins School and had befriended Laura Bridgman. Anagnos described the 21-year-old Sullivan as "exceedingly intelligent, strictly honest, industrious." He also suggested to the Kellers that she would make an "excellent instructress and a most reliable guide" for Helen.

Annie was the daughter of poor Irish immigrants. As a young girl, she had contracted an eye disease that left her with less and less sight as she got older. At age 9, her parents abandoned her, sending her to the state poorhouse in Tewksbury, Massachusetts. There, among the crippled, insane, alcoholic, and elderly, she lived in her own world of darkness for more than 5 years.

Then, one day in 1880—the year Helen Keller was born—the State Board of Charities ordered a thorough investigation of the horrible living conditions that were common at Tewksbury. When the investigating committee arrived at the poorhouse, a nearly blind, illiterate girl—Annie Sullivan—threw herself on the floor at the feet of the officials and pleaded, "I want to go to school."

After her parents abandoned her when she was 9 years old, Annie Sullivan lived in a Massachusetts poorhouse under horrible conditions.

Annie was removed from the poorhouse and sent to the Perkins School. During the school's vacation periods, she worked at a boardinghouse in Boston. One of the lodgers there helped her find a surgeon at Massachusetts Eye and Ear Infirmary. Through a series of operations, the surgeon restored enough of her sight so Annie could read for short periods of time.

At the Perkins School, Annie flourished. She had limited sight, but the school's administrators felt she could not live on her own. They allowed her to stay until 1886, when she graduated first in her class. Although she could neither read nor write at age 14, when she graduated at age 20 she could read and write letters and braille—the special alphabet for the blind that uses touch and raised dots. She could also fingerspell.

Exhausted from weeks of reading about Laura Bridgman's education and from her long train ride, Annie Sullivan arrived in Tuscumbia, Alabama, on March 3, 1887. She was there to begin what she thought was a $25-per-month teaching job. She was unaware that it was to become both her life's work and her greatest passion.

Into the Light

Annie Sullivan knew from her own first-hand experience of living in the poorhouse the frustration of being an intelligent girl without an education. She could only imagine how difficult it must be for a 6-year-old not to be able to see, hear, or speak, and to be alone in a world cut off from human communication.

She had learned from reading about the education of Laura Bridgman how difficult it was to create a bond with a severely disabled child. Having such a child learn to trust, and maybe even to love, a teacher was an enormous task.

21

Annie left Boston with a mixture of sadness and excitement. But for the children of the Perkins School, her journey was the stuff of dreams. They pooled their allowance money to buy a doll for Helen. Laura Bridgman herself, a skilled seamstress, sewed a set of clothes for the doll.

Annie patterned her teaching method after Samuel Howe's work with Laura Bridgman. First, she would spell a word onto Helen's hand, then demonstrate the word's meaning by giving her an object or making an action.

The first word Annie spelled into Helen's hand was *doll*. She illustrated the word by giving Helen the doll she had brought from the children at the Perkins School.

Although Helen immediately liked the "game," and made her fingers dance in Annie's palm, she had no idea that Annie was making words, or that words even existed. Helen continued to play the "fingerspelling game" for weeks.

Annie continued to "talk" to Helen all the time by spelling words into her hand—the same way that parents constantly talk to babies. This steady communication is how babies learn to make sounds and

Fingerspelling was the best means of communication between young Helen and her teacher.

then to speak. Annie was also teaching her young student about obedience and manners. They moved to the cottage less than two weeks after Annie arrived, and Helen progressed there. Annie's strict approach to teaching Helen was starting to pay off. For the first time in Helen's life, she had a teacher who was at once firm, loving, and consistent.

At one point, Annie taught Helen to crochet, and Helen was able to relax and concentrate on this task. Helen would sit and crochet, while Annie wrote notes of her teaching and letters to Michael Anagnos and her friends back in Boston.

The first real learning breakthrough had happened at the water pump, when Helen came to the realization that each set of motions Annie made in the palm of her hand actually had meaning.

From that day on, Helen awoke with a purpose in life, to learn all that she could about the world and the people around her. "Teacher" could not keep up with the little girl as she ran from one object to another asking for more and more knowledge.

After a few weeks, Helen and Annie moved back into the main house. The young girl now had an impressive vocabulary of about 300 words that she could spell in Annie's hand. Young Helen could even create short, simple sentences.

"Teacher" could not keep up with the little girl as she ran from one object to another asking for more and more knowledge.

Rather than treating Helen as a 6-year-old being educated, Annie treated her more as a toddler first learning language. The educational system of the late 19th century focused on children learning by memorization. To Annie, this method assumed that "every child is a kind of idiot who must be taught to think." But from watching Helen, Annie could see that the best kind of education was one that allowed a child to learn naturally, as an infant does. "If a child is left to think for himself, he will think more and better," Annie wrote in her notes.

Helen's concept of language grew every day. When Annie told her that squirrels came to drink at a particular stream, Helen named the spot "squirrel cup." She learned by doing, by exploring. She touched every flower, and quickly learned to tell the different varieties by the feel of the stem and the petals. Annie also helped by spelling the names of the different flowers in Helen's hands.

25

During Helen's first summer with Annie, she learned to read and write using the braille alphabet.

In late May, Annie began teaching Helen the alphabet. First, she would spell a letter in her palm, then she would run the girl's finger over a card with a large, raised letter on it. Within a few days, Helen knew the entire alphabet. Then she began moving the cards around to make simple words. By July, she was reading the simple books of raised letters that Annie had brought from Boston. Before the summer was over, Annie had written to Michael Anagnos at the Perkins School requesting more materials.

In July, Annie began to teach Helen the braille alphabet. In 1826, Louis Braille, a French teacher of the blind, developed this system of raised dots. Each set of dots represents a letter or letter combination. Letters are created in stiff paper using a sharp instrument called a stylus. By poking the stylus into the paper, the dots appear raised on the other side and can be read by feel with the fingertips.

Helen liked braille better than the letter alphabet. With braille, she could read what she had just written. Although she handwrote letters, and later typed letters and manuscripts using the letter-alphabet, Helen wrote in braille throughout her life.

The story of Helen Keller and her miracle teacher captured many people's imaginations. By 1888, the Boston press was writing stories about the little girl in Alabama who was rescued from a lifetime of darkness through the efforts of a Perkins School graduate. In May, Helen, her mother, and Annie, went to Boston to visit the school at Michael Anagnos's invitation. On their way, they stopped in Washington, D.C., to visit and thank Alexander Graham Bell, and to meet with President Grover Cleveland, who had invited them to the White House.

In 1888, Helen, Annie, and Helen's mother were invited to the White House to meet Grover Cleveland.

For the next four winters, Helen and Annie traveled to Boston and lived as Anagnos's guests at the Perkins School. In addition to teaching Helen, Annie instructed others how to teach blind-and-deaf children. She also helped bring a blind-and-deaf five-year-old boy to the Perkins School.

In 1890, Annie and Helen were told that in Europe, blind-and-deaf children were being taught to speak. Helen promptly spelled "I must speak" into Annie's hand. She did learn, although it was hard. Few could understand her deep and toneless voice.

Helen's First Writings

In 1892, Helen wrote a short essay about herself called "My Story," that the editor of *The Youth's Companion* had requested. For this she earned $100. At that time, her father's businesses were failing, and he could no longer afford Annie's salary.

Alexander Graham Bell, who had always liked Helen, invited her to visit Washington, D.C. They went to the zoo and to President Cleveland's second Inaugural Ball. Bell also asked her to speak to the American Association to Promote the Teaching of Speech to the Deaf, for which she received a fee.

There, Annie met two men who were setting up a new school in New York for deaf students. Bell got his friend, John Spaulding—a wealthy and generous Boston businessman—to pay Helen's tuition to the new school. There, she learned lip-reading, as well as academic subjects such as arithmetic, geography, French, and German. When Spaulding died a few years later, Bell and the famous writer Mark Twain raised the funds for her to stay in school.

Helen set her sights on college, and she set her sights high. She wanted to attend Radcliffe College, the women's division of Harvard University in Cambridge, Massachusetts. Shortly after her father's death in 1896, she applied to the Cambridge School for Young Ladies, a preparatory school for those girls hoping to attend Radcliffe.

The school's director pleaded that he had no facilities to handle a blind-and-deaf 16-year-old and her companion. But, as soon as he met Helen, he accepted her. While at the Cambridge School, she learned math, Greek and Roman history,

With the help of Alexander Graham Bell and famous writer Mark Twain, Helen attended a new school in New York where she learned many subjects.

Alexander Graham Bell and Mark Twain helped Helen get an education.

Because she could not see or
hear, Helen relied on touch to
communicate with Annie.

French, German and Latin, and literature. She left
the school after one year, however, because of a dis-
agreement between Annie and the director. The
next year, she and Annie lived in Wrentham,
Massachusetts, while Helen studied with a tutor. In
1899, Helen took and passed the entrance exam for
Radcliffe College.

Helen began college in the fall of 1900, and
graduated with her class in the spring of 1904.
During that time, she also wrote her first book, *The
Story of My Life*. The book started as a magazine
article for *Ladies Home Journal*. Helen originally
didn't want to write for the magazine, but the editor
kept telling her only she could write the true story of
her life. The editor offered Helen $3,000—more
than most Americans made in one year. For a young
woman looking for a way to support herself, it was
impossible for her to turn down such an offer. Her
article marked the beginning of Helen's career as a
writer, lecturer, and fundraiser. In the years to come,
Helen's writings would give the world a special look
inside the life of a young girl who had been trans-
formed. Her story would bring inspiration and hope
to millions who faced similar challenges.

○ ○ ○ ○ ○ **4** ○ ○ ○ ○ ○

"The Story of My Life"

The Story of My Life received wonderful reviews, and was translated into nearly 50 languages. It is still read today. Money earned from the book's royalties allowed Helen and Annie to buy a farmhouse in Wrentham, Massachusetts, where they moved after Helen's graduation from Radcliffe.

The book also brought John Macy into Helen and Annie's life. A young English instructor at Harvard, and an editor for *The Youth's Companion*, Macy was hired by *Ladies Home Journal* to assist Helen and Annie with a four-part magazine article.

Macy soon became a part of the household and the three enjoyed each other's company a great deal. Macy learned to fingerspell, and his reading and rereading Helen's manuscript helped reduce the strain on Annie's eyes. Annie had worked hard for years, fingerspelling lectures into Helen's hands and reading her assignments. Now, she was nearly 40 and her eyesight was beginning to worsen again. Macy proposed to Annie that they marry, but she refused, knowing that Helen needed her. But Helen knew that Annie, who had denied herself a personal life for nearly 20 years, was in love.

Annie Takes a Husband

In 1905, Annie married Macy, and became Annie Sullivan Macy. Her new husband assured her that he would not come between her and Helen. The three lived together at the farmhouse. Macy continued to work for *The Youth's Companion* and to write a book about Edgar Allen Poe. Helen wrote another book, *The World I Live In*, published in 1908, in which she told how she used her other senses to make up for being blind and deaf.

In 1909, John Macy joined the Socialist party. So did Helen. The party's principles for equality, such as women's right to vote, appealed to Helen. Inspired

In 1905, Annie married John Macy, an editor who had helped Helen with her writings.

by these ideas Helen published *Out of the Dark*, a collection of essays about social problems, in 1913.

The book was not very popular. While everyone wanted to read about what Helen Keller had to go through in her life, few wanted to read about her political ideas for social change.

Money was increasingly tight for the three at the Wrentham farmhouse. And Annie and John's marriage was having problems. John was becoming a heavy drinker and Annie's health and sight were failing. It was clear that the marriage would soon end.

Helen and Annie set out on a lecture tour in order to earn money, and Helen finally accepted a generous offer from the millionaire businessman Andrew Carnegie. Carnegie offered to give Helen a $5,000-per-year pension for as long as she lived.

Though Helen had continued to take speech lessons, she was still very difficult to understand. Nevertheless, she soon became a successful speaker. With Annie at her side explaining their early years and interpreting her remarks for the audience, Helen spoke publicly often and traveled extensively. The two eventually hired a young Scottish woman, Polly Thomson, to run their household. Polly booked the lectures, made arrangements, and cared for the two women and their home when they were away.

Helen and Annie lectured until 1916, when Helen's outspoken opposition to World War I caused her to lose most of her speaking engagements. They went home, nearly broke, and had to sell the house in Wrentham. Annie was also ill, and went off for a time with Polly to look after her, first to upstate New York and then to Puerto Rico. Helen, now 36 years old, went home to Alabama to spend some time with her mother.

When Annie and Helen were reunited the next year, they moved to a small house on Long Island, and started looking for things to do. They earned some money by making a documentary film of Helen's life, but it did not do particularly well. Finally, Helen and Annie took the tale of their meeting and of Helen's early education to the vaudeville stage. But vaudeville was a combination of theater and circus, hardly an appropriate setting for such a story. Still, the steady work earned the partners the money they needed to live.

After her marriage to John Macy, Annie lived with her husband and Helen at the farmhouse in Wrentham.

In order to make money and support themselves, Helen and Annie performed a stage version of their life together.

Helen and Annie performed on the vaudeville stage on-and-off from 1919 until 1924. During that time, Helen's mother died.

By 1924, Annie was often ill, always tired, and almost completely blind. She could no longer put up with the demands of one-night appearances. To earn a steady living, and to focus on the true mission of her life—helping the blind—Helen accepted an offer from the American Foundation for the Blind (AFB) to become a fundraiser. Finally, Helen would be doing work that she truly found fulfilling.

39

○ ○ ○ ○ ○ **5** ○ ○ ○ ○ ○

Helen Keller, Humanitarian

Although Helen Keller only worked for the American Foundation for the Blind for a short time, it was the start of a 35-year career as a fundraiser and humanitarian. During that time, she spoke out for the rights of—and needs of—the physically disabled and raised money for numerous charities.

In her three years with the AFB, she raised over $1 million, a huge amount of money in the 1920s. Contributions ranged from a few dollars sent in by children, to thousnds of dollars donated by wealthy businesssmen. The cowboy and humorist Will Rogers made a series of radio broadcasts on Helen's behalf and donations poured into the AFB.

Helen and Annie toured the country, speaking to over 250,000 people in more than 100 cities.

Throughout the 1920s, Helen also made public appeals for one standard alphabet for the blind, instead of the five different alphabets that were used in that day. By 1932, publishers and educators for the blind throughout the world agreed to use the original French braille alphabet as their standard.

Helen also continued writing books, again about herself. In 1927, she wrote about her spiritual growth in *My Religion*. In 1929, she published the second part of her autobiography, *Midstream*. Helen also made the first of her many journeys to Europe to speak, traveling with both Annie and Polly Thomson.

For the next few years, the pace slowed. Annie became more frail. Helen continued to advise the AFB, and to make appearances for charities.

In 1936, Annie died. Many people thought that mourning her companion of 50 years would make Helen retire from public life. But she felt that there was still much work to be done. In 1937, she made her first trip to Asia, having been asked by the director of the Lighthouse for the Blind in Osaka, Japan, to come and work with his organization. Helen and Polly gave 97 lectures in 39 Japanese cities, in what was to be the first of many world tours.

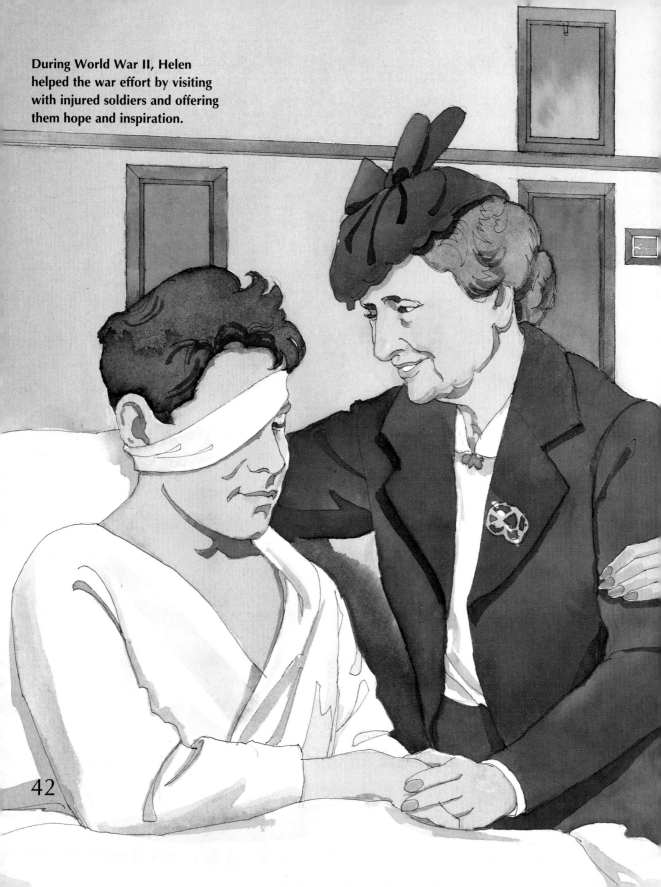

During World War II, Helen helped the war effort by visiting with injured soldiers and offering them hope and inspiration.

42

Each time, Helen spoke of the needs of the disabled and raised money for a host of charities.

When they returned to the United States, Helen and Polly moved into a new home, in Westport, Connecticut, that had been bought for her by the AFB. There she began to write her biography of Annie Sullivan.

During World War II, Helen was asked to help the war effort by visiting soldiers who had been blinded or deafened in battle. She traveled the country, going to military hospitals, often with First Lady Eleanor Roosevelt, who's husband, Franklin, was president.

Before her death in 1968, Helen managed to finish her biography of her longtime friend, partner, and teacher, Annie Sullivan.

After the war, Helen and Polly continued touring hospitals and schools for the disabled around the world, visiting 35 countries on five continents. Helen stopped her world traveling in 1957. After Polly's death in 1960, Helen rarely left her Westport home. A stroke in 1961 left her unable to travel. After 7 years of limited movement and discomfort, Helen finally died in 1968, at age 88.

Despite all her traveling during the 1940s and 1950s, Helen managed to finish her biography of Annie. In 1955, she published *Teacher: Anne Sullivan Macy*. In the book, Helen wrote of Annie:

> She was a lively young woman whose imagination was kindled by her accomplishments with little Helen to unique dreams of molding a deaf-blind creature to the full life of a useful, normal human being...It was no chance that freed Helen's mind but a prophet's vision and the gift of a born teacher quickening the brain with inner fire.

It was that "fire" of Annie Sullivan's that enabled Helen to write those words. And it was the poetic talent of Helen Keller that brought those words to life. Together, these two women gave the world hope and inspiration that will last forever.

Glossary

autobiography A story about a person's life written by that person.

braille A system of writing and printing that consists of letters made up of raised dots.

disability A physical or mental impairment that makes it difficult for a person to learn or to do something.

fingerspelling A method of communicating by making symbols for letters against the palm of the hand.

illiterate The inability to read or write.

infirmary A place where sick people go for care and treatment.

lecturer A person who gives a speech or presentation to an audience.

sign language A method of communicating by using hand gestures instead of speech to convey meaning.

stroke A sudden weakness or paralysis caused by a rupture or blockage of blood vessels in the brain.

stylus An instrument used to write on soft materials, such as paper or wax; a sharp instrument used to create braille.

vaudeville Stage entertainment consisting of various acts that was popular in the United States during the late 19th and early 20th century.

Further Reading

Bergman, Thomas. *Finding a Common Language: Children Living with Deafness.* Milwaukee, WI: Gareth Stevens, 1989.

Birch, Beverly. Louis Braille: *Bringer of Hope to the Blind.* Milwaukee, WI: Gareth Stevens, 1991.

Charlip, Remy and Miller, Mary B. Handtalk: *An ABC of Finger Spelling & Sign Language.* New York: Macmillan, 1984.

Graff, Stewart and Graff, Polly A. *Helen Keller: Toward the Light.* New York: Chelsea House, 1992.

Hall, Candace C. Shelley's Day: *The Day of a Legally Blind Child.* Newington, CT: Andrew Mountain Press, 1980.

Hunter, Edith F. *Child of the Silent Night: The Story of Laura Bridgman.* Boston: Houghton Mifflin, 1963.

Kudlinski, Kathleen V. *Helen Keller.* New York: Puffin Books, 1991.

Sullivan, Mary B., et. al. *A Show of Hands: Say It in Sign Language.* New York: HarperCollins Children's Books, 1985.

Wilkie, Katharine E. *Helen Keller: From Tragedy to Triumph.* New York: Macmillan, 1986.

Index